Look what I can colour

out and about

Illustrated by Marie Allen

www.autumnchildrensbooks.co.uk

Colour the picture.

Follow the number key to colour the picture.

1 2 3 4 5 6

Trace the coloured lines to
finish the picture.

Colour the big picture to match
the little picture.

Colour the picture.

Follow the number key to colour the picture.

1 2 3 4 5 6

Trace the coloured lines to
finish the picture.

Colour the big picture to match
the little picture.

Colour the picture.

Follow the number key to colour the picture.

1 2 3 4 5 6

Trace the coloured lines to
finish the picture.

Colour the big picture to match
the little picture.

Colour the picture.

Follow the number key to colour the picture.

1 2 3 4 5 6

Trace the coloured lines to
finish the picture.

Colour the big picture to match the little picture.

Colour the picture.

Follow the number key to colour the picture.

1 2 3 4 5 6

Trace the coloured lines to
finish the picture.

Colour the big picture to match
the little picture.

Colour the picture.

Follow the number key to colour the picture.

1 2 3 4 5 6

Trace the coloured lines to
finish the picture.

Colour the big picture to match
the little picture.

Colour the picture.

Follow the number key to colour the picture.

1　2　3　4　5　6

Trace the coloured lines to
finish the picture.

Colour the big picture to match
the little picture.

Colour the picture.

Follow the number key to colour the picture.

1 2 3 4 5 6

Trace the coloured lines to
finish the picture.

Colour the big picture to match
the little picture.

Colour the picture.

Follow the number key to colour the picture.

1 2 3 4 5 6

Trace the coloured lines to
finish the picture.

Colour the big picture to match
the little picture.

Colour the picture.

Follow the number key to colour the picture.

1 2 3 4 5 6

Trace the coloured lines to finish the picture.

Colour the big picture to match
the little picture.

Colour the picture.

Follow the number key to colour the picture.

1 2 3 4 5 6

Trace the coloured lines to
finish the picture.

Colour the big picture to match
the little picture.

Colour the picture.

Follow the number key to colour the picture.

1 2 3 4 5 6

Trace the coloured lines to
finish the picture.

Colour the big picture to match the little picture.

Colour the picture.

Follow the number key to colour the picture.

Trace the coloured lines to
finish the picture.

Colour the big picture to match
the little picture.

Colour the picture.

Follow the number key to colour the picture.

Trace the coloured lines to finish the picture.

Colour the big picture to match
the little picture.

Colour the picture.

Follow the number key to colour the picture.

Trace the coloured lines to
finish the picture.

Colour the big picture to match
the little picture.

Colour the picture.

Follow the number key to colour the picture.

1 2 3 4 5 6

Trace the coloured lines to
finish the picture.

Colour the big picture to match
the little picture.

Colour the picture.

Follow the number key to colour the picture.

1 2 3 4 5 6

Trace the coloured lines to
finish the picture.

Colour the big picture to match
the little picture.

Colour the picture.

Follow the number key to colour the picture.

1 2 3 4 5 6

Trace the coloured lines to finish the picture.

Colour the big picture to match the little picture.

Colour the picture.

Follow the number key to colour the picture.

1 2 3 4 5 6

Trace the coloured lines to
finish the picture.

Colour the big picture to match
the little picture.

Colour the picture.

Follow the number key to colour the picture.

1 2 3 4 5 6

Trace the coloured lines to
finish the picture.

Colour the big picture to match
the little picture.

Colour the picture.

Follow the number key to colour the picture.

(1) (2) (3) (4) (5) (6)

Trace the coloured lines to finish the picture.

Colour the big picture to match the little picture.

Colour the picture.

Follow the number key to colour the picture.

1 2 3 4 5 6

Trace the coloured lines to
finish the picture.

Colour the big picture to match the little picture.

Colour the picture.

Follow the number key to colour the picture.

1 2 3 4 5 6

Trace the coloured lines to
finish the picture.

Colour the big picture to match the little picture.

Colour the picture.

Follow the number key to colour the picture.

1 2 3 4 5 6

Trace the coloured lines to finish the picture.

Colour the big picture to match
the little picture.

Colour the picture.

Follow the number key to colour the picture.

1 2 3 4 5 6

Trace the coloured lines to
finish the picture.

Colour the big picture to match
the little picture.

Colour the picture.

Follow the number key to colour the picture.

1 2 3 4 5 6

Trace the coloured lines to finish the picture.

Colour the big picture to match
the little picture.

Colour the picture.

Follow the number key to colour the picture.

1 2 3 4 5 6

Trace the coloured lines to
finish the picture.

Colour the big picture to match the little picture.

Colour the picture.

Follow the number key to colour the picture.

1 2 3 4 5 6

Trace the coloured lines to
finish the picture.

Colour the big picture to match
the little picture.

Colour the picture.

Follow the number key to colour the picture.

1 2 3 4 5 6

Trace the coloured lines to
finish the picture.

Colour the big picture to match
the little picture.

Colour the picture.

Follow the number key to colour the picture.

1 2 3 4 5 6

Trace the coloured lines to
finish the picture.

Colour the big picture to match
the little picture.

Colour the picture.

Follow the number key to colour the picture.

1 2 3 4 5 6

Trace the coloured lines to
finish the picture.

**Colour the big picture to match
the little picture.**

Colour the picture.

Follow the number key to colour the picture.

1 2 3 4 5 6

Trace the coloured lines to
finish the picture.

Colour the big picture to match
the little picture.

Colour the picture.

Follow the number key to colour the picture.

1 2 3 4 5 6

Trace the coloured lines to
finish the picture.

Colour the big picture to match the little picture.

Colour the picture.

Follow the number key to colour the picture.

1 2 3 4 5 6

Trace the coloured lines to finish the picture.

Colour the big picture to match
the little picture.

Colour the picture.

Follow the number key to colour the picture.

1 2 3 4 5 6

Trace the coloured lines to
finish the picture.

Colour the big picture to match
the little picture.

Colour the picture.

Follow the number key to colour the picture.

1 2 3 4 5 6

Trace the coloured lines to finish the picture.

Colour the big picture to match
the little picture.

Colour the picture.

Follow the number key to colour the picture.

1 2 3 4 5 6

Trace the coloured lines to
finish the picture.

Colour the big picture to match
the little picture.

Colour the picture.

Follow the number key to colour the picture.

1 2 3 4 5 6

Trace the coloured lines to finish the picture.

Colour the big picture to match
the little picture.

Colour the picture.

Follow the number key to colour the picture.

1 2 3 4 5 6

Trace the coloured lines to
finish the picture.

Colour the big picture to match
the little picture.

Colour the picture.

Follow the number key to colour the picture.

① ② ③ ④ ⑤ ⑥

Trace the coloured lines to finish the picture.

Colour the big picture to match
the little picture.

Colour the picture.

Follow the number key to colour the picture.

1 2 3 4 5 6

Trace the coloured lines to
finish the picture.

Colour the big picture to match
the little picture.

Colour the picture.

Follow the number key to colour the picture.

1   2   3   4   5   6

Trace the coloured lines to finish the picture.

Colour the big picture to match
the little picture.

Colour the picture.

Follow the number key to colour the picture.

1 2 3 4 5 6

Trace the coloured lines to
finish the picture.

Colour the big picture to match
the little picture.

Colour the picture.

Follow the number key to colour the picture.

1 2 3 4 5 6

Trace the coloured lines to
finish the picture.

Colour the big picture to match
the little picture.

Colour the picture.

Follow the number key to colour the picture.

1 2 3 4 5 6

Trace the coloured lines to
finish the picture.

Colour the big picture to match the little picture.

Colour the picture.

Follow the number key to colour the picture.

1 2 3 4 5 6

Trace the coloured lines to finish the picture.

Colour the big picture to match
the little picture.

Colour the picture.

Follow the number key to colour the picture.

1 2 3 4 5 6

Trace the coloured lines to
finish the picture.

Colour the big picture to match
the little picture.

Colour the picture.

Follow the number key to colour the picture.

Trace the coloured lines to
finish the picture.

Colour the big picture to match
the little picture.

Colour the picture.

Follow the number key to colour the picture.

1 2 3 4 5 6

Trace the coloured lines to
finish the picture.

Colour the big picture to match
the little picture.

Colour the picture.

Follow the number key to colour the picture.

1 2 3 4 5 6

Trace the coloured lines to
finish the picture.

**Colour the big picture to match
the little picture.**

Colour the picture.

Follow the number key to colour the picture.

1 2 3 4 5 6

Trace the coloured lines to
finish the picture.

Colour the big picture to match the little picture.

Colour the picture.

Follow the number key to colour the picture.

1 2 3 4 5 6

Trace the coloured lines to finish the picture.

Colour the big picture to match the little picture.

Colour the picture.

Follow the number key to colour the picture.

1 2 3 4 5 6

Trace the coloured lines to
finish the picture.

Colour the big picture to match
the little picture.

Colour the picture.

Follow the number key to colour the picture.

1 2 3 4 5 6

Trace the coloured lines to
finish the picture.

Colour the big picture to match
the little picture.

Colour the picture.

Follow the number key to colour the picture.

1 2 3 4 5 6

Trace the coloured lines to
finish the picture.

Colour the big picture to match the little picture.

Colour the picture.

Follow the number key to colour the picture.

Trace the coloured lines to
finish the picture.

Colour the big picture to match the little picture.

Colour the picture.

Follow the number key to colour the picture.

1 2 3 4 5 6

Trace the coloured lines to
finish the picture.

Colour the big picture to match
the little picture.

Colour the picture.

Follow the number key to colour the picture.

1 2 3 4 5 6

Trace the coloured lines to
finish the picture.

Colour the big picture to match
the little picture.

Colour the picture.

Follow the number key to colour the picture.

1 2 3 4 5 6

Trace the coloured lines to finish the picture.

Colour the big picture to match
the little picture.

Colour the picture.

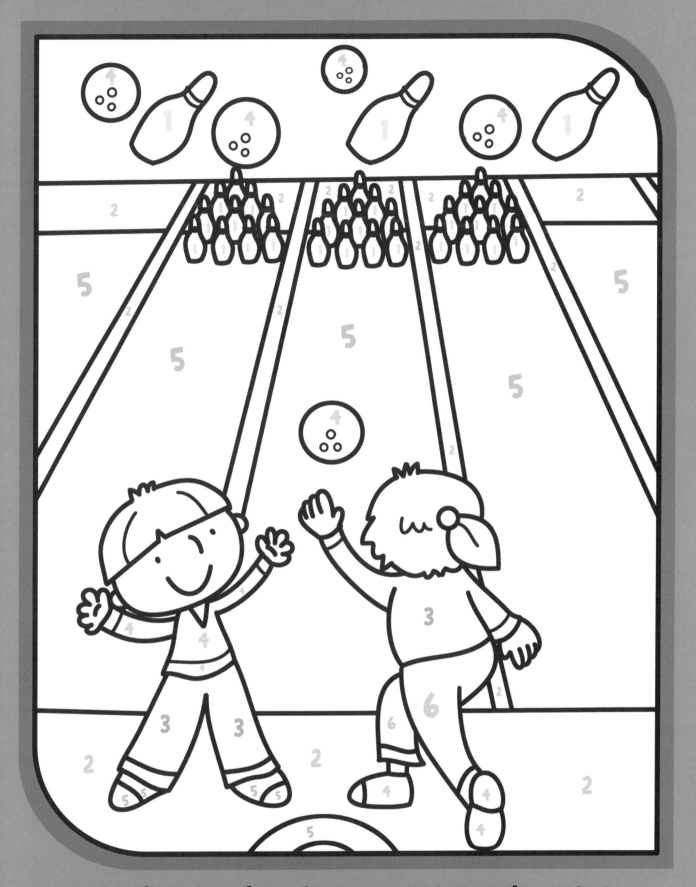

Follow the number key to colour the picture.

1 2 3 4 5 6

Trace the coloured lines to
finish the picture.

Colour the big picture to match
the little picture.

Colour the picture.

Follow the number key to colour the picture.

1 2 3 4 5 6

Trace the coloured lines to
finish the picture.

Colour the big picture to match
the little picture.

Colour the picture.

Follow the number key to colour the picture.

Trace the coloured lines to
finish the picture.

Colour the big picture to match
the little picture.

Colour the picture.

Follow the number key to colour the picture.

1 2 3 4 5 6

Trace the coloured lines to
finish the picture.

Colour the big picture to match
the little picture.

Colour the picture.

Follow the number key to colour the picture.

1 2 3 4 5 6

Trace the coloured lines to
finish the picture.